BUTTERFLIES AND MOTHS

LEVEL 1 READER

READING LEVEL
K - GRADE 1

Written by Kathryn Knight

The CREATIVE EDGE name is a trademark of Dalmatian Publishing Group,
Franklin, Tennessee 37068-2068. 1-800-815-8696.
No part of this book may be reproduced or copied in any form without written permission
from the copyright owner. CE12987/0610

Flowers with Wings

The world is full of
butterflies and moths.
Some are small.
Some are huge!
Some are gray.
And some are so colorful,
they look like flying flowers.

You may see butterflies in your garden in the daytime. Most moths fly at night. Have you ever seen moths around your porch light?

How Are They Alike?

Butterflies and moths are insects.

They have six legs.

They have three body parts.

They have two feelers.

And they have four wings.

How Are They Different?

A moth's body is often thicker than the body of a butterfly. A moth's feelers may be more feathery than butterfly feelers.

When a butterfly is resting, it folds its wings up.

When a moth is resting, its wings lie flat, close in to its sides.

From Egg to Adult

Moths and butterflies start
out the same way—
as a tiny egg.

butterfly caterpillar   moth caterpillar

A caterpillar hatches from the egg.
The caterpillar eats leaves. Lots of leaves!
It grows and grows and GROWS!

Then the caterpillar makes a case
to live in for a while.

A butterfly case
is a *chrysalis*.
(**kriss**-uh-liss)

A moth case
is a *cocoon*.
(kuh-**koon**)

Inside the case, a big change takes place.
The caterpillar turns into an adult.

Many Kinds and Colors

Butterflies and moths come
in all sizes and colors.
They are amazing to watch!

How Big Are Butterflies?

Most butterflies are about 3 inches wide.

The smallest are half an inch wide.
These tiny butterflies flitter
from wildflower to wildflower.

Birdwing butterflies are the largest.
They can be 9 to 12 inches wide!

How Big Are Moths?

Most moths are 1 or 2 inches wide.

The smallest are the
leaf miner moths.
They are only as long
as a grain of rice.

Atlas moths are the largest.
They can be 9 to 12 inches wide.
That is as big as a bird!

The Great Traveler

Many birds fly south for the winter.
But did you know that there are
butterflies that fly south, too?
Monarch (**mah**-nark) butterflies
travel all the way to Mexico
to be warm in the winter.
In spring, they fly thousands
of miles north until they
reach cooler fields.

Don't Eat Me!

Monarchs lay eggs
on milkweed plants.
Their caterpillars love
to eat milkweed.
The milkweed makes
them taste terrible, so
birds stay away from them!

This is the viceroy butterfly.
Birds won't eat viceroys
because they *look* like monarchs.
Can you tell the difference?

The leaf butterfly looks just like small, dried leaves. It is able to hide from birds and reptiles by blending in with leaves.

This moth looks just like tree bark! Do you think a bird would see it?

Swallowtails

Some of the most beautiful butterflies are the swallowtails. Their two lower wings look like the tail of a swallow bird.

Swallowtails like to visit gardens.
They sip sweet juices from flowers.
A swallowtail's tongue is a long straw.
Slurp!

Moths of the Moon

Some moths also have wing "tails."
These beautiful moths come out at night.
Most are called luna or moon moths.
Have you ever seen a green luna moth?
They can be 4 inches wide!

Luna Moth

Indian Moon Moth

Comet Moth

Spanish Moon Moth

Sunset Moth

How did the postman butterfly get its name?
People saw that it went to the same
spots every day—just like a postman.

This is called a
zebra butterfly.
Do you see why?

Doesn't this look like a hummingbird?
It's a moth! A hummingbird moth!

Look closely.
Do you see why
it's called a dogface
butterfly?

This moth glides at night.
It is so huge, it can be scary.
It is a white witch moth.

Living Flowers

The next time you are in a garden, sit still.
Watch to see if a butterfly visits a flower.
Maybe, if you sit *very* still,
it will land on *you*.
Enjoy.